Green Bay Packers
Titletown Trivia Teasers

Cover photo by Mike DeVries/The Capital Times

Green Bay Packers

Titletown Trivia Teasers

Don Davenport

PRAIRIE OAK PRESS
Black Earth, Wisconsin

Library of Congress Control Number: 2004109181
ISBN: 1-879483-93-9

Photos: Vernon J. Biever and Mike DeVries/The Capital Times

Printed in the United States of America by Sheridan Books

08   07   06   05   04   5 4 3 2 1

Contents

Quarterback Brett Favre.   Mike Devries photo.

CHAPTER ONE

A Super Bowl, but No Cigar
1997–'98

Although Coach Holmgren repeatedly warned players and fans against letdowns and complacency after the Super Bowl XXXI victory, there was talk of a 19-0 season by the time summer training camp began.

But dreams of an unbeaten season ended with Game 2, when the Philadelphia Eagles nipped the Pack 10-9. Game 11 saw the Packers suffer a humiliating 41-38 loss to the 0-10 Indianapolis Colts, but they bounced back the following week to end an eight-game losing streak to the Dallas Cowboys, winning 45-17.

By the end of the season, the Packers were 13-3, Brett Favre had become the NFL's only three-time MVP, sharing honors with Detroit's Barry Sanders, and the Pack was headed for the playoffs and Super Bowl XXXII.

Regular Season Play

Q. The Farve–Sanders tie for 1997 MVP honors was the second in the 41-year history of the award. When was the first tie, and who were the co-winners?

A. 1960; Philadelphia quarterback Norm Van Brocklin and Detroit linebacker Joe Schmidt shared the award.

Q. On December 28, 2003, Ahman Green (RB, 2000-) rushed for 218 yards against Denver, setting a franchise record. Who held the Packers' single game rushing record until then?

A. Dorsey Levens (RB, 1994-97) rushed for 190 yards against Dallas on November 23, 1997.

Q. The '97 season marked the first time in Packer history that two receivers surpassed the 1,000 yard mark. Who were they?

A. Antonio Freeman (WR, 1995-97) with 1,243 yards and Robert Brooks (WR, 1992-97) with 1,010 yards.

Q. What NFL career record did Brett Favre set in Game 14 against Tampa Bay?

A. He became the first player in NFL history to throw 30 or more TD passes in four consecutive seasons.

Q. The Packers failed to score a touchdown in the 10-9 loss to the Eagles. When was the last time they failed to score a touchdown?

A. September 13, 1992, in a 31-13 loss to Tampa Bay.

Q. In Game 3 of the '97 season, the Pack finally defeated a team against which they had been 0-8. Which team was it?

A. The Miami Dolphins.

Q. Brett Favre scored his 153rd career TD toss in Game 4 against the Minnesota Vikings, breaking the Packer record of 152 career TDs held by the revered Bart Starr (QB, 1956-71). Favre broke the record in 83 regular season games. How long did it take Starr to set his record?

A. 191 games.

The Playoffs

Q. With the Packers' 21-7 playoff victory over Tampa Bay on January 4, 1998, Mike Holmgren became the second NFL coach to win at least one playoff game in five straight seasons (1993-97). Who was the first?

A. John Madden, whose Oakland Raiders won playoff games from 1973-77.

Q. Brett Favre's second quarter TD pass to Antonio Freeman in the Packers' 23-10 playoff victory over San Francisco on January 11, 1998, set a Packer record for completed TD passes in consecutive postseason games, which was?

A. Eight. Bart Starr held the previous record of TD passes in six consecutive playoff games.

Q. Under Coach Mike Holmgren, how many times has Green Bay knocked San Francisco out of the playoffs?

A. Three. January 6, 1996 (27-17), January 4, 1997 (35-14) and January 11, 1998 (23-10).

Super Bowl XXXII

With Green Bay was favored by two touchdowns, Denver sporting an 0-4 Super Bowl record, and the NFC winning the last 13 Super Bowls, the Packers looked like a shoo-in for Super Bowl XXXII. But it was not to be.

Despite Brett Favre's three TD passes, the Pack seemed flat, while Denver, hoping to finally give aging QB John Elway (0-3 in Super Bowl appearances) a win, was mile-high.

The end result: Denver 31, Green Bay 24.

After thinking it over, Brett Favre described the game as "a wake up call." But Green Bay fans could only mutter the time-honored saw, "wait 'til next year."

Q. Which Packer receivers caught Favre's three TD passes?

A. Antonio Freeman (WR) two, and Mark Chmura (TE, 1993-97) one.

Q. By defeating Green Bay, Denver became only the second wild-card team to win a Super Bowl; who was the first?

A. The 1980 Oakland Raiders.

Q. Counting his years as San Francisco quarterbacks coach and offensive coordinator, how many Super Bowls has Mike Holmgren coached in?

A. Four. Super Bowl XXIII and XXIV with the 49ers, and Super Bowl XXXI and XXXII with the Packers.

Q. What is Holmgren's record as a Super Bowl coach?

A. 3-1, for a winning percentage of .750.

Q. Who was named Super Bowl XXXII's MVP?

A. Denver running back Terrell Davis, who rushed for 157 yards and three TDs.

CHAPTER TWO

Super Season, Super Bowl
1996–'97

Picked by many as Super Bowl contenders even as summer training camp began, the 1996 version of the Green Bay Packers romped through the season like a team destined for glory.

Indeed, they were.

Led by Coach Mike Holmgren, a low-key, Harley-riding family man with a wry sense of humor and strong sense of history, the Packers fielded the league's most prolific offense and stingiest defense. And provided a thrill-a-minute as one player after another stepped forward and carved his name into the record books and franchise history.

When it was over, the Green Bay Packers were the World Champions—a title won with old-fashioned virtues like teamwork, dignity, fellowship, love, and hard, hard work.

And Green Bay, Wisconsin, was once again Titletown USA, fulfilling a goal Packer fans had dreamed of for a generation. How sweet it was.

Regular Season Play

Q. The Packers were the NFL's top scoring team in 1996 with how many points?

A. A total of 456, an average of 28.5 per game.

Q. The Pack also led the NFL in allowing the least points for the season. How many points did they allow?

A. Only 210, an average of 13.1 per game.

Q. The last team to lead the NFL in both points scored and fewest points allowed in a season went undefeated. Which team was it?

A. The 1972 Miami Dolphins, who were 17–0.

Q. The '96 Packers' defense led the NFL in fewest yards allowed—4,156. When was the last time the Packers led the league in fewest yards allowed?

A. In 1967, the year of their last title.

Q. How many touchdowns did the Packers' defense allow in '96?

A. Only 19, the NFL's lowest total ever in a 16-game season.

Q. Who led the Packers in tackles in '96?

A. George Koonce (LB, 1992–96) had 69 solo tackles and 28 assists for a total of 97.

Q. How many rushing first downs did the Packers give up in '96?

A. Seventy-four, the fewest the team has ever permitted in a 16-game season.

Q. Desmond Howard (WR, 1996) set a punt-return record in '96; what was it?

A. Howard had 58 returns for 875 yards, an NFL record for punt-return yardage.

Q. How many punts did Howard return for TDs?

A. Three in the regular season: 65 yards against San Diego (Game 3); 75 yards against Chicago (Game 13); 92 yards against Detroit (Game 15). Howard's 92-yard return was the fourth longest in Packers' history.

Q. Who became the first player in 21 years to lead the Packers in rushing yardage for three consecutive seasons?

A. Edgar Bennett (RB, 1992–96) was the Packers' rushing leader in 1994, '95 and '96.

Q. Before Bennett, who was the last player to rush for 1,000 yards or more in three consecutive seasons?

A. John Brockington (RB, 1971–77) led the team in rushing in 1971, '72 and '73.

Q. In his 66th NFL game (Game 1 against Tampa Bay), Brett Favre (QB, 1992–96) passed for 247 yards and tied Joe Namath as the third fastest quarterback to reach 15,000 passing yards. Which two quarterbacks did it in fewer games?

A. Dan Marino (56) and Jim Everett (64).

Q. Five pairs of Packers on the '96 team, all unrelated, shared the same last name. Can you name them?

A. Gary and Gilbert Brown; Earl and Santana Dotson; Calvin and Sean Jones; Eugene and Michael Robinson; Brian and Tyrone Williams.

Q. Quarterback Brett Favre set an NFC record when he threw 39 touchdown passes in regular season play. Who was the previous record holder?

A. Favre broke his own record. He threw 38 TD passes in 1995.

Q. In setting those records, how many interceptions did Favre throw?

A. A total of 26.

Q. How many passes did Andre Rison (WR, 1996) catch in his first game with the Packers?

A. Rison caught five passes for 44 yards in his Green Bay debut against St. Louis.

Q. The Packers were 13–3 in the '96 season. When was the last time the Green and Gold won 13 regular season games?

A. In 1962, when they were 13–1.

Q. Which team gave the Packers that lone 1962 defeat?

A. The Detroit Lions, who won a Thanksgiving Day game, 26–14.

Q. Who holds the Packers' record for most passes attempted in a single game?

A. Brett Favre, who passed 61 times in the Pack's 23–20 overtime win against San Francisco in Game 7. Favre had 28 completions, two interceptions, and one touchdown.

Q. Who is the only Green Bay Packer to win the NFL's Most Valuable Player Award in two consecutive years?

A. QB Brett Favre was named MVP in 1995 and 1996. (Go stand in the corner if you missed this one).

Q. Who was second to Favre in the 1996 MVP balloting?

A. Denver QB John Elway.

Q. Which other Packers have been named the NFL's MVP?

A. Paul Hornung (RB, 1957–62, 64–66), Jim Taylor (FB, 1958–66), and Bart Starr (QB, 1956–71).

Q. Only two players on the Packers' '96 roster were with the team when Ron Wolf took over as General Manager in 1991. Who were they?

A. Kicker Chris Jacke (drafted 1989) and safety LeRoy Butler (drafted 1990).

Q. How many players on the '96 roster were Packers' first round draft picks?

A. Four: Wayne Simmons (LB, 1993); Aaron Taylor (G, 1994); Craig Newsome (CB, 1995); John Michels (T, 1996).

Q. In what game was Brett Favre held without a TD pass?

A. Game 7, the second game against Tampa Bay.

Q. Through 1996, how many consecutive games had the Packers won at Lambeau Field?

A. Eighteen.

Q. How many of those victories came in 1996?

A. Ten: against Philadelphia, San Diego, San Francisco, Tampa Bay, Detroit, Chicago, Denver, and Minnesota in the regular season, San Francisco in the NFC Divisional Title Game, and Carolina in the NFC Championship Game.

Q. In how many games in '96 regular season play did Brett Favre throw four touchdown passes?

A. Five—against Tampa Bay, Seattle, Chicago, Detroit, and Denver.

Q. How many rushing touchdowns did Favre score in regular season play?

A. Two: In Game 13 against Chicago (one yard) and in Game 15 against Detroit (one yard).

Q. How many QB sacks did the Packers' defense have in '96?

A. Seventy-seven, made by 11 different players.

Q. Who was the Packers's QB sack leader in 1996?

A. Reggie White (DE, 1993–96), with 8.5 sacks.

Q. How many pass interceptions did the Packers' defense make in '96?

A. Twenty-six, spread among 10 players.

Q. Who led the team in pass interceptions in '96?

A. Eugene Robinson (S, 1996), with six.

Q. Three Packers' defenders ran interceptions back for TDs. Who were they?

A. LeRoy Butler (S, 1990–96), Doug Evans (CB, 1993–96), and George Koonce.

Q. Of the three, who made the longest interception run back for a touchdown?

A. LeRoy Butler intercepted a Stan Humphries pass in Game 3 against the San Diego Chargers and ran it back 90 yards for a TD.

Q. How many takeaways did the Packers have in '96?

A. Thirty-nine: 26 interceptions and 13 fumbles.

Q. Chris Jacke (K, 1989–96) was the Packers' leading scorer in 1996 with 114 points—51 extra points and 21 field goals. Who was the second leading scorer?

A. Keith Jackson (TE, 1996) and Dorsey Levens tied for second, each scoring 10 TDs for 60 points.

Q. Favre threw to 13 different receivers in '96. How many scored TDs?

A. Ten.

Q. Which Packers' receiver had the most touchdowns?

A. Keith Jackson (TE, 1996) turned 40 receptions into 10 TDs.

Q. What was the longest TD pass Favre threw in the '96 season?

A. Don Beebe (WR, 1996) had an 80-yard TD reception in Game 4 against Minnesota—the longest in regular season play.

Q. Kicker Chris Jacke (1989–96) set an NFL record in '96. What was it?

A. Jacke's 53-yard field goal to beat San Francisco 23–30 in overtime (Game 7) was the longest overtime field goal in NFL history.

The Playoffs

Q. In the NFC Divisional Playoff Game, which Green Bay player had more yards in punt returns than San Francisco did rushing?

A. Desmond Howard, who had 117 yards in punt returns. The 49ers had 68 yards rushing.

Q. A record crowd of 60,787 attended the NFC Divisional Playoff Game at Green Bay. How many no-shows were there?

A. Three.

Q. Desmond Howard made his forth punt return of the season for a touchdown barely two minutes into the first quarter of the NFC Divisional Playoff Game against San Francisco. How far was it?

A. Seventy-one yards.

Q. The NFC Championship Game at Lambeau Field wasn't exactly "Ice Bowl II," as predicted, at least not by Green Bay standards. What was the temperature at game time?

A. Three degrees.

Q. Edgar Bennett's touchdown in the NFC Championship Game against the Carolina Panthers set a record, which was?

A. It was Bennett's fourth postseason rushing TD, a Packers' record.

Q. What is the name of the trophy that is awarded to the National Football Conference champion?

A. The George Halas Trophy, named in honor of the founder of the Chicago Bears.

Super Bowl XXXI
January 26, 1997

Q. The Packers and Patriots set a Super Bowl record in the first quarter of the game; what was it?

A. The combined 24 points scored by the two teams made it the highest scoring first quarter in Super Bowl history.

Q. How many members of the Packers' Super Bowl XXXI starters were drafted by the Pack?

A. Thirteen.

Q. Desmond Howard's kickoff return in the third quarter of Super Bowl XXXI set a record, which was?

A. The 99-yard return was the longest in Super Bowl history and the longest in NFL postseason history.

Q. Howard set another kickoff return record. What was it?

A. His 38.5-yard kickoff-return average (154 yards on four returns) was a new Super Bowl record.

Q. Howard's third return record was?

A. His combined 244 return yards (154 yards in four kickoff returns) were a Super Bowl record.

Q. Who were the TV game announcers for Super Bowl XXXI?

A. Pat Summerall (play-by-play) and John Madden (commentary).

Q. The Super Bowl champion takes home the Vince Lombardi Trophy. What is the trophy awarded to the game's most valuable player called?

A. The Pete Rozell Trophy.

Q. Who won the Pete Rozell Trophy in Super Bowl XXXI?

A. Packers' wide receiver Desmond Howard.

Q. In receiving the MVP award, Howard set a Super Bowl first. What was it?

A. He was the first special teams player in Super Bowl history to receive the award.

Q. Desmond Howard was the fourth Heisman Trophy winner to capture Super Bowl MVP honors; who were the others?

A. Roger Staubach (Cowboys, Super Bowl VI), Jim Punkett (Raiders, Super Bowl XV), and Marcus Allen (Raiders, Super Bowl XVIII).

Q. Who was the only player on the '96 Packers' squad to have previously played on a winning Super Bowl team?

A. Jim McMahon (QB, 1995–96), who led the Chicago Bears to victory over the New England Patriots in Super Bowl XX (1986).

Q. How many members of the Packers' Super Bowl XXXI team were over 30?

A. Ten.

Q. One member of the Patriots' Super Bowl XXXI team began the '96 season with the Packers. Who was he?

A. Mike Bartrum, Patriots' backup tight end and special-teams player. Bartrum, who was with the Packers in 1995, was sent to the Patriots in August, 1996.

Q. One player on the Packer's Super Bowl XXXI roster began the '96 season with the New England Patriots. Who was he?

A. Jeff Dellenbach, backup center and snapper on field goals and extra points. After playing for the University of Wisconsin, Dellenbach spent 10 years with Miami and played with New England in 1995. He was waived by the Pats on September 10 and signed by the Packers on December 3.

Q. Which 1996 Packers' player had appeared in four previous Super Bowls?

A. Don Beebe played in Super Bowls XXV, XXVI, XXVII, and XXVIII with the Buffalo Bills (all losses).

Q. How many players on the Packers' Super Bowl roster were picked up in 1996 from teams that eventually made the playoffs?

A. Five: Don Beebe (WR), Carolina Panthers; Bruce Wilkerson (T), Desmond Howard (WR), and Andre Rison (WR), Jacksonville Jaguars; Jeff Dellenbach (C), New England Patriots.

Q. Green Bay was the first NFC Central Division Champion to reach the Super Bowl in 11 years. The last Central Division team in the Super Bowl also defeated the New England Patriots. Who were they?

A. The Chicago Bears. They downed the Patriots 46–10 in Super Bowl XX, also held in New Orleans.

Q. While Super Bowl XXXI was the Packers' and Patriots' first postseason meeting, the two teams had met five times before in regular season play. Which team holds the series record?

A. New England: the Pats won meetings in 1973 (33–24, Foxboro); 1985 (26–20, Foxboro); and 1994 (17–16, Foxboro). The Packers won in 1979 (27–14, Green Bay) and 1988 (45–3, Milwaukee). The Pack also won the 1996 preseason opener for both clubs (24–7, Green Bay).

Q. How many QB sacks did Reggie White have in Super Bowl XXXI?

A. Three, a Super Bowl record.

Q. White is the NFL's all-time QB sack leader. How many sacks did he have at the end of the 1996 season?

A. A total of 168.5.

Q. Brett Favre's scoring strike to Antonio Freeman in the second quarter of Super Bowl XXXI was the longest TD pass in Super Bowl history. How much territory did it cover?

A. Eighty-one yards.

Q. What color jerseys did the Packers wear in Super Bowl XXXI?

A. Green. The Packers were designated the home team and chose green for their third Super Bowl appearance.

Q. On January 17, 1997, the Packers announced that 60,000 Lambeau Field seats would be sold by telephone for a January 27 "Return to Titletown" celebration honoring the Packers after Super Bowl XXXI. How many phone inquiries about tickets were received?

A. One and one-half million.

Ted Fritsch running wide right in old City Stadium, Green Bay (East High School).
Vernon J. Biever photo.

CHAPTER THREE

Early Years
The 1920s and '30s

One of the few 19th-century "town teams" to make it into professional football, and the only publicly-owned team in professional sport, playing in the smallest city to have a National Football League franchise, the Green Bay Packers are truly the stuff of which legends are made.

Founded by player / coach E.L. "Curly" Lambeau and *Green Bay Press-Gazette* sports editor Gorge W. Calhoun, the Packers fielded their first professional team in 1921, with a roster made up of players nicknamed Cub, Tubby, Curly, Toody, Jab, and Cowboy. Playing home games on a vacant lot in a city park, and passing the hat among spectators to help defray expenses, the Packers won six NFL Championships in 31 seasons under Curly Lambeau's guiding hand.

Over all, the Green Bay Packers have won more NFL titles than any other team in league history. Their history is filled with a tradition of great plays, great players, and great rivalries that have shaped the very fabric of the game of professional football.

Q. How much did the Green Bay Packers' NFL franchise cost?

A. $50. The document is on display at the Green Bay Packer Hall of Fame.

Q. What is the Packers' record for the number of tie games played in a single season?

A. Three.

Q. In how many seasons did they have three ties?

A. Three: 1922, 1926, and 1928.

Q. In those nine games, the Packers tied one team three times. Which team was it?

A. The Chicago Bears: 6–6 and 3–3 in 1926, 12–12 in 1928. The other ties: 1922, 0–0, Milwaukee Badgers, 0–0, Rock Island Independents, 3–3, Racine Legion; 1926, 0–0 Duluth Eskimos; 1928, 0–0, New York Yankees; 7–7 Providence Steamroller.

Q. The Packers-Detroit Lions Thanksgiving Day games in the '50s and '60s were legendary. Who was the Pack's first league opponent in a Thanksgiving Day contest?

A. The Hammond (IN) Pros, in a game played in Green Bay on November 29, 1923. The Packers won 19–0.

Q. Who was the Packers' first ever preseason opponent?

A. The Chicago Boosters, a semi-pro team. The game was played on September 25, 1921; the Pack won, 13–0.

Q. The Packers swept the Chicago Bears in 1935, winning 7–0 on September 22 and 17–14 on October 27. How long was it before the Pack swept the Bears again?

A. Twenty-six years. The 1961 Packers defeated the Bears 24–0 at Green Bay and 31–28 at Chicago.

Q. Who is the Packers' all-time scoring leader?

A. Ryan Longwell (K, 1997-) had scored 844 points by the end of the 2003 season, his seventh with the Packers. He broke the legendary Don Hutson's record of 823 points in 11 seasons (1935-45).

Q. Which Packer player became the only man inducted into both the Pro Football Hall of Fame and the Pro Baseball Hall of Fame?

A. Robert (Cal) Hubbard (T, 1929–33, '35). Hubbard was an American League umpire for 17 years after his football career ended.

Q. Who holds the Packers' record for the longest run from scrimmage?

A. Ahman Green scampered for a 98-yard TD against Denver on December 28, 2003, breaking the record of Andy Uram (HB, 1938-43) who scored a 97-yard TD run against the Chicago Cardinals on October 8, 1939.

Q. What is the record number of passes the Packers have had intercepted in a postseason game?

A. Six, in the 1939 NFL Championship Game against the New York Giants.

Q. Where did the Packers play their first home games?

A. From 1919 through 1923, the Pack played home games at Hagemeister Park in Green Bay.

Q. What position did Earl L. (Curly) Lambeau, the Packers' founder and coach, play for the team?

A. Lambeau played halfback for the Packers from 1919 through 1929.

Q. In what year did the Packers play their first "home" game in Milwaukee and who was their opponent?

A. In 1933. The Pack lost to the New York Giants, 10–7.

Q. Where in Milwaukee was that game played?

A. State Fair Park.

Q. When did the Packers play their first College All-Star game?

A. In 1937. They lost to the collegians 6–0, becoming the first professional team to lose the College All-Star Game.

Q. Between 1921 and 1940, the Packers lost by more than 30 points only once. To which team was that?

A. The Pottsville Maroons downed the Pack 31–0 in 1925.

Q. Where did the Packers play their 1923 and 1924 home games?

A. Bellevue Park in Green Bay. Hagemeister Park was dug up in 1923 to build a new East High School.

Q. The 1922–24 NFL roster listed three Wisconsin pro football teams. The Packers were one, who were the other two?

A. The Milwaukee Badgers and Racine Legion. The Legion did not play in 1925 and in 1926 played as the Racine Tornadoes. Neither team played after 1926.

Q. The Packers were shut out 20–0 on the last game of the 1921 season. Who was their opponent?

A. The Chicago Staleys, who in 1922 became the Chicago Bears.

Q. How many players from the University of Wisconsin were on the Packers' 1921 team?

A. Two: Howard (Cub) Buck (T, 1921–25) and Jim Cook (G, 1921).

Q. Who holds the Packers' career touchdown record?

A. Don Hutson, who scored 105 touchdowns in 11 seasons with the Packers.

Q. How many touchdown passes did Hutson catch?

A. Ninety-nine.

Q. Green Bay became the first team to win three consecutive NFL titles. In which years did they accomplish this?

A. In 1929, '30, and '31.

Q. In the early years of the NFL, league championships were won on the basis of winning percentage points. When did the Packers play their first ever postseason game?

A. In 1936.

Q. Who was their opponent in that game?

A. The Boston (now Washington) Redskins. The Packers won the NFL Championship 21–6 at the Polo Grounds in New York.

Q. When were the Green Bay Packers founded?

A. Although Green Bay fielded town teams as early as 1896, the generally-accepted date for the Green Bay Packers birth is August 14, 1919.

Q. How did the team get the nickname, "Packers?"

A. The 1919 city team was sponsored by the Indian Packing Company, thus "Packers."

Q. The 1919 Packers out scored their opponents 565–12 and had a 10–1 record against teams from Wisconsin, Michigan and Illinois. Which team beat them?

A. A Beloit team fielded by Fairbanks-Morse Co. downed the Packers 6–0 on November 23, 1919.

Q. Still a town team in 1920, the Packers were sponsored by the Acme Packing Company (who bought out Indian Packing), and were 9–1–1 for the season. To which team did they suffer their lone loss?

A. Again it was Beloit who defeated the Packers 14–3 on November 14, 1920.

Q. Which Green Bay player threw Don Hutson his first touchdown pass as a Packer?

A. Arnie Herber (B, 1930–40).

Q. When did the Packers play their first professional game and who was the opponent?

A. The Packers' first pro game was played on October 23, 1921. They defeated the Minneapolis Marines 7–6.

Q. Other than the Chicago Bears, the Packers did not play another team that is currently active in the NFL under the same name until 1928. Who was that team?

A. The New York Giants. The Packers met them for the first time at Green Bay on October 7, 1928, losing to the defending NFL champs 6–0.

Q. In 1929, Curly Lambeau brought three future Pro Hall of Fame players to the Packers. Who were they?

A. August (Mike) Michalske (G, 1929–35, 37), Robert (Cal) Hubbard, and Johnny (Blood) McNally (B, 1929–33, 35–36).

Q. In 1930, the Packers played their first game against the Portsmouth Spartans, a team with which they continue to have an intense rivalry, although under a different name. What current NFL team did the Spartans become?

A. The Detroit Lions (1934).

Q. How many touchdowns and total points did Don Hutson score in his rookie year?

A. Hutson, scored seven touchdowns and 43 points in 1935.

Q. The 1933 season marked a milestone in Green Bay Packers' history. What was it?

A. The Packers were 5–7–1, their first losing season in franchise history.

Q. The Packers beat the Chicago Bears for the first time on September 21, 1924, but the game has never been recognized by the NFL. Why?

A. It was played before the season officially opened. The NFL considers September 28 as the start of the '24 season.

Q. What is the largest number of fumbles the Packers have had in postseason play?

A. Four, in the 1938 Championship Game against the New York Giants. The record was equalled in the 1982 Second-Round Playoff Game against the Dallas Cowboys. Not surprisingly, the Packers lost both games.

Q. The NFL introduced its draft of college players in 1936. Who was the Packers' first ever draft pick?

A. Guard Russ Letlow, of San Francisco, who played for the Packers from 1936 to 1942 and in 1946.

Q. Which Packers' player has led the team in rushing attempts for the most seasons?

A. Clarke Hinkle (FB, 1932–41) led the Packers in rushing attempts for eight seasons: 1932–34 and 37–41.

Q. Which Green Bay Packer holds the record for leading the team in rushing touchdowns for the most consecutive seasons?

A. The record of five consecutive seasons is shared by Verne Lewellen (B, 1927–31) and Ted Fritsch (FB, 1943–47).

Q. Which man scored the most touchdowns?

A. Lewellen scored 31 TDs, Fritsch 30.

Q. Which Green Bay Packer led the team in pass receiving yards gained for the most consecutive seasons?

A. Don Hutson led the Pack in pass receiving yards gained for 11 seasons (1935–45), every year he played pro football.

Q. What is the least number of first downs the Packers have had in a postseason game?

A. Seven, against the Boston Redskins in the 1936 NFL Championship Game. Regardless, the Packers won 21–6.

Q. What is the largest number of rushing attempts made by the Packers in a single postseason game?

A. Fifty-two, against the New York Giants in the 1939 NFL Championship Game. Green Bay won, 27–0.

Q. When did Curly Lambeau retire as an active Packers' player?

A. Lambeau hung up his cleats at the end of the '29 season, having thrown 24 touchdown passes in his nine-year playing career with the Packers.

Q. The NFL was divided into the Eastern and Western Division for the first time in 1933. Beside Green Bay, which other teams were in the Western Division?

A. The Chicago Bears, Portsmouth Spartans, Cincinnati Reds, and Chicago Cardinals.

Q. In 1934, the Packers defeated a team that played under two different names. Who was it?

A. The Cincinnati Reds, who played the last three games of the season as the St. Louis Gunners. The Packers trounced the Reds 41–0 on October 14 and the Gunners 21–14 on December 12.

Q. The 1935 Packers lost three regular season games to one team . Who was it?

A. The Chicago Cardinals. The Cards downed the Packers 7–6 on September 15, 3–0 on October 13, and 9–7 on November 28.

Q. The 1931 Packers set a scoring record that stood for 30 years. What was it?

A. They scored 44 touchdowns, a record that stood until the 1961 Packers scored 49.

Q. How did Packers' back Johnny (Blood) McNally acquire his nickname?

A. While playing semi-pro football in college, McNally took the name "Blood" from a popular film of the era, "Blood and Sand," thus becoming Johnny Blood.

Q. Which Green Bay player was elected to political office still playing with the Packers?

A. Verne Lewellen, a law school graduate from Nebraska, was elected to the Brown County (Wis.) district attorney's post in 1929. He played for the Packers until 1932.

Q. Who threw the first professional football pass to the legendary Don Hutson?

A. Bobby Monnett (B, 1933–38) threw the first pass to Hutson in the 1935 season opener against the Chicago Cardinals. The pass was incomplete.

Q. What is the fewest number of passes the Packers have attempted in a single game?

A. The Packers threw no passes in 17–0 victory over the Portsmouth Spartans on October 8, 1933.

Q. Including postseason games, what is the Packers' longest consecutive streak without a loss?

A. Twenty-three (1928–30), when they were 21–0–2.

Q. Which Green Bay player later became head coach of the University of Miami Hurricanes?

A. Howard (Cub) Buck (T, 1921–25). While playing for the Packers, Buck coached at Lawrence University in Appleton, purchased an Appleton auto dealership, and was an executive for the Boy Scouts of America. He retired in 1926 to coach the Hurricanes.

Q. Don Hutson's 1935 contract was so large that Packer officials set up two bank accounts to keep the Alabama star's salary a secret in depression-era Green Bay. Was it:

a. $500 per game?
b. $250 per game?
c. $175 per game?

A. Hutson received $175 per game.

Q. In the late 1930s, two brothers from Minnesota played for the Packers at the same time. Who were they?

A. George Svendsen (C, 1935–37, 40–41) and Earl (Bud) Svendsen (C, 1937, 39). George played on the 1936 championship team, while Earl played with the champions of 1939.

Max McGee takes it downfield against the Rams in a 1954 game at State Fair Park, Milwaukee. Vernon J. Biever photo.

CHAPTER FOUR

Forgotten Years
The 1940s and '50s

The 1940s and '50s marked good times and bad for the Green Bay Packers. There were soaring highs—a fourth NFL Championship, the team's first thousand-yard rusher—and searing lows that included some of the worst seasons and worst defeats in Green Bay history.

A number of Packers' stars of the '30s reached the end of their careers and left the game in the mid-'40s, including Don Hutson, Joe Laws, Buckets Goldenberg, and Charley Brock. In 1949, with the team struggling financially and Curly Lambeau watching games from the press box, the Packers were 2–10–0. Amid a loud hue and cry for a coaching change, Lambeau resigned, on January 31, 1950, although he continued coaching in the NFL.

The 1950s brought the Packers a string of losing seasons led by a parade of losing coaches. Still, there were glimmers of better days ahead. Tobin Rote, Babe Parilli, Bill Howton, Bob Mann, and Billy Grimes brought excitement to an otherwise dreary decade.

By the late '50s, players named McGee, Ringo, Gregg, Starr, Hornung, and Kramer had been added to the roster. In 1959, the Packers hired their fourth head coach in a decade. Although no one yet realized it, Green Bay's salvation was at hand—in the unlikely form of a gap-toothed Italian-American disciplinarian named Vincent Thomas Lombardi.

Q. Who was the first Packers' player to rush for 1,000 yards or more in a single season?

A. Tony Canadeo (HB, 1941–44, 46–52) rushed for 1,052 yards in 208 attempts in 1949 (12 games)—only the third NFL player to rush for 1,000 yards or more.

Q. Who led the Packers in scoring in the 1949 season?

A. Ted Fritsch (FB, 1942–50), who scored one TD, 11 points after touchdown and five field goals for a total of 32 points.

Q. How long was the shortest game the Packers ever played?

A. One hour, 45 minutes.

Q. Who was Packers' opponent in that game?

A. The Detroit Lions. The game was played at Detroit on November 17, 1946. Green Bay won, 9–0.

Q. The Packers have played two other games that lasted less than two hours. Who were their opponents?

A. In both cases, the Detroit Lions. The Packers' second ever shortest game, one hour and 50 minutes, was played against the Lions at Detroit on October 25, 1942; Green Bay won, 28–7. The Packers and Lions played a one-hour, 52-minute game at Detroit on December 2, 1945; the Lions won, 14–3.

Q. The present Packers' stadium opened on September 29, 1957, but was not named Lambeau Field until 1965. What was it called before then?

A. New City Stadium. It was renamed Lambeau Field after the death of founder Curly Lambeau.

Q. Which Packers' coach has the worst ever won-loss record?

A. Ray (Scooter) McLean, who coached the Packers to a dismal 1–10–1 season in 1958.

Q. Which team did the Packers defeat in that '58 season?

A. The lone victory was a 38–35 win over the Philadelphia Eagles.

Q. Which Packers' player scored the most receiving touchdowns in his rookie season?

A. Bill Howton (E, 1952–58) scored 13 touchdowns in 1952, making 53 catches for 1,231 yards.

Q. Who holds the Packers' highest punt return average for a single season?

A. Billy Grimes (HB, 1950-52). In 1950 Grimes returned 29 punts for 555 yards and a 19.1 yard average per return.

Q. Who holds the Packers' record for the longest kickoff return?

A. Al Carmichael (HB, 1953–58) returned a kickoff for 106 yards on October 7, 1956.

Q. Against which team did Carmichael make that record run?

A. The Chicago Bears.

Q. What is the shortest completed touchdown pass in Packers' history?

A. Four inches.

Q. Who threw the pass and who caught it?

A. The Cecil Isbell (QB, 1938–42) to Don Hutson pass came in the Packers' 45-28 victory over the Cleveland Rams on October 18, 1942.

Q. Which Packer player caught the most passes in a single game?

A. Don Hutson caught 14 passes for 134 yards against the Giants at New York on November 22, 1942.

Q. Which Packers' quarterback holds the team record for throwing touchdown passes in the most consecutive games?

A. Brett Favre has passed for TD's in 25 consecutive games: weeks 9-17, 2002 and weeks 1-16, 2003, breaking the record of quarterback Cecil Isbell (1938-42).

Q. In how many consecutive games did Isbell throw TD's?

A. Twenty-two—in every regular season game in 1941 and 1942.

Q. Who was the Green Bay Packers' first African-American player?

A. Bob Mann (E, 1950–54). He was inducted into the Packers Hall of Fame in 1988.

Q. What is the largest margin of defeat ever suffered by the Packers?

A. Fifty-six points.

Q. Which team administered that trouncing?

A. The Baltimore Colts, who stomped the Packers 56–0 at Baltimore on November 2, 1958.

Q. Which Packer player threw the most pass interceptions in a single game?

A. Tom O'Malley (QB, 1950) threw six interceptions in 15 attempts against the Detroit Lions on September 17, 1950. Detroit won 45–7 and O'Malley's career with Green Bay was over.

Q. Which Packers' quarterback threw the most touchdown passes in his rookie season?

A. Vito (Babe) Parilli (1952–53, 57–58) threw 13 TD passes in 1952.

Q. Until Brett Favre completed a 99-yard TD pass in 1995, what was the longest touchdown pass ever thrown by a Packer QB?

A. Tobin Rote (1950–56) threw a 96 yard pass to Billy Grimes in a game at San Francisco on December 10, 1950.

Q. Which Packers' quarterback holds the record for most pass completions in his NFL rookie season?

A. Tobin Rote completed a record 83 passes in 1950.

Q. Which Packers' quarterback gained the most yards passing in his NFL rookie season?

A. Babe Parilli threw for 1,416 yards in 1952.

Q. Which Packers' quarterback became the first in NFL history to throw for 2,000 yards in a single season?

A. Cecil Isbell threw for 2,021 yards in 1942. His 24 TD passes that season were also an NFL record.

Q. Which Packers' player holds the NFL record for scoring the most points in one quarter of play?

A. Don Hutson caught four touchdown passes and kicked five extra points, scoring 29 points in the second quarter of the of the Packers-Detroit game at Milwaukee on October 7, 1945. It is an NFL record that still stands today.

Q. When did the Packers play their first televised game?

A. October 24, 1953.

Q. Who was their opponent in that game?

A. The Pittsburgh Steelers, who won the Saturday night game 31–14.

Q. Who was the only Packers' coach to be dismissed while a season was in progress?

A. Gene Ronzani was released by the Packers on November 27, 1953, with two weeks remaining in the regular season.

Q. Who took over as coach after Ronzani was dismissed?

A. Assistants Ray (Scooter) McClean and Hugh Devore took over as co-coaches. The Packers went 2–9–1 for the season.

Q. In 1950, the Packers changed their team colors to green and gold. What were the uniform colors before then?

A. Navy blue and gold.

Q. Which player won the 1949 Wisconsin State Baseball League batting championship while a member of the Green Bay Packers?

A. Earl "Jug" Girard (QB, 1948–51). A No. 1 draft pick from the University of Wisconsin, Girard, who played in the NFL for 10 years, played semi-pro baseball for the Green Bay Bluejays during his four years with the Packers.

Q. In the decade of the '40s (1940–49) only three players led the Packers in rushing. Who were they?

A. Clark Hinkle (FB, 1932–41) in 1940 and '41; Ted Fritsch, in 1942, '44, and '45; Tony Canadeo in 1943 and 1946–49.

Q. In the same decade, only two players led the Packers in scoring. Who were they?

A. Don Hutson, 1940–45 (587 total points) and Ted Fritsch, 1946–49 (217 total points).

Q. In 1949, with the team in dire financial straits, the Packers took an unusual fund-raising step. What was it?

A. They played a Thanksgiving intrasquad game in Green Bay that drew 15,000 fans and raised $50,000.

Q. Which '50s quarterback was the Packers' rushing leader in three of his seven seasons with the team?

A. Tobin Rote led the Packers in rushing in 1951 (523 yards, 3 TDs); 1952 (313 yards, 2 TDs); and 1956 (398 yards, 11 TDs). In his career with the Green and Gold, Rote rushed for 2,205 yards in 419 attempts, scored 29 TDs, and had three 100-yard rushing games. He ranks tenth on the Packers' all-time rushing list.

Q. The 1953 Packers struggled to a 2–9–1 season, tying the Chicago Bears and defeating one team twice. Who was that team?

A. The Baltimore Colts. The Packers defeated the Colts 37–14 at Green Bay and 35–24 at Baltimore. The 72 points scored against the Colts represented 36 percent of the Packers' total output.

Q. In 1954, a fifth-round draft choice from Tulane caught 36 passes for 614 yards and scored nine TDs in his rookie season with the Packers. He became one of the best-known team members during the Lombardi era. Who was he?

A. Max McGee (WR, 1954, 57-67) caught 345 passes for 6,346 yards and 50 touchdowns in 12 seasons with Green Bay. He ranks 6th among the team's top 20 career receivers.

Q. McGee, who was also the Packers' punter, was called into the military in 1955. Who replaced him?

A. Coach Lisle Blackbourn brought in Dick Deschine (1955–57) to replace McGee. Although he didn't play college ball, Deschine averaged more than 42 yards per kick in three years with the Packers.

Q. What is Max McGee's first name?

A. William.

Q. In what year were hash marks first added to Green Bay's City Stadium?

A. The stripes were added in 1955 to aid ball placement.

Q. Which team holds the record for gaining the most yards rushing against the Packers in a single game?

A. The Los Angeles Rams, who on December 16, 1956, gained 611 yards and thrashed the Packers 49–21.

Q. November 18, 1956 marked the end of an era in Packer history when the team played their final game in old City Stadium. Who did the Packers play on this memorable occasion?

A. The San Francisco 49ers, who took advantage of three Green Bay fumbles in the last quarter to forge a 17–16 victory.

Q. Green Bay's New City Stadium was inaugurated on September 29, 1957. What world-famous politician spoke at the dedication ceremonies?

A. Then Vice President Richard Nixon.

Q. Who was the Packers' opponent in the first game at the new stadium and who won the game?

A. The Chicago Bears. The Packers won, 21–17.

Q. Who was the first Packers' quarterback to complete more than 100 passes in a single season?

A. Cecil Isbell completed 117 passes in 1941.

Q. On October 7, 1945, the Packers scored 57 points—a team record that stands to this day. Against which team did they set that record?

A. The Detroit Lions, who lost to the Packers 57–21.

Q. Despite being shut out twice in the 1944 season, the Packers won the NFL Championship. Which teams shut them out?

A. The Chicago Bears, 21–0 at Chicago, and the New York Giants, 24–0 at New York.

Q. Who did the Packers play in the 1944 NFL Championship Game?

A. The New York Giants. The Packers redeemed the early season loss by winning the title game, 14–7.

Q. Joe Laws (RB, 1934–45) set an individual record in the 1944 Championship Game that still stands today. What was it?

A. Laws intercepted three Giants' passes, the most ever by a Packers' player in a postseason game.

Q. The last three players from Green Bay's championship teams of 1936, 1939, and 1944 retired in December, 1945. Who were they?

A. Don Hutson, the NFL's all-time leading receiver (488 passes, 99 touchdowns) Joe Laws, and Buckets Goldenberg, who held the Packers' longevity record to that point (13 years).

Q. Curly Lambeau, the only coach the Packers had known, resigned in early 1950. After he left Green Bay, Lambeau coached two other NFL teams. Who were they?

A. The Chicago Cardinals (1950–51) and Washington Redskins (1952–53).

Q. In 1949, Lambeau's last season as head coach, the Packers were 2–10. How many non-losing seasons did they have between then and 1959, when Vince Lombardi was hired as head coach?

A. Two. The Packers were 6–6 in 1952 and 1955, and did not have another winning season until Lombardi arrived.

Q. What is the fewest number of pass completions the Packers have had in a postseason game?

A. Three, in the 1944 NFL Championship Game against the New York Giants.

Q. How many touchdown passes did Bart Starr throw in his first year with the Packers?

A. Two. Backing up starter Tobin Rote, Starr threw 44 passes in 1956, completing 24 for 325 yards. He was intercepted three times.

Q. Despite a 3–9–0 record in 1951, the Packers threw a then-record 478 passes, completing 231 for 2,846 yards. Who were the quarterbacks on the '51 team?

A. Tobin Rote and Bobby Thomason (1951).

Q. When was the first time the Packers finished a season in last place?

A. In 1949, when the team was 2–10–0.

Q. Two Packer standouts of the '40s were related. Who were they?

A. Charlie Brock (C / LB, 1939–47) and Lou Brock (B, 1940–45) were cousins. Charlie was the Packers' second-round draft pick in 1939, Lou was a second-round pick in 1940.

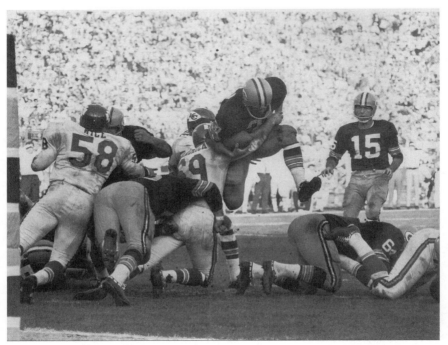

Jim Taylor goes up and over against the Kansas City Chiefs in Super Bowl I. Bart Starr is No. 15. Vernon J. Biever photo.

CHAPTER FIVE

The Lombardi Era
The 1960s

When in 1959 the Green Bay Packers hired Vincent T. Lombardi, a former New York Giants assistant, as head coach, no one on the planet could have imagined that a legend was about to be born, or that professional football history was in the making.

Lombardi's first year as coach produced the Packers' first winning season in 12 years. In nine years under Lombardi, the Packers' fortunes soared to undreamed of heights—nine consecutive winning seasons, including NFL championships and Super Bowl victories. Lombardi's Packers still hold team and NFL records.

Lombardi stepped down as the Packers' coach at the end of Super Bowl II, but stayed on as general manager. He left Green Bay at the end of the 1968 season to become head coach and general manager of the Washington Redskins, and coached Washington to a winning season in 1969.

Vince Lombardi died of cancer on September 3, 1970. He was 57 years old.

Q. How many NFL Championships did the Packers win under Coach Vince Lombardi?

A. Five.

Q. Four of the Packers' championship game victories during the Lombardi era came at the expense of two teams. Who were they?

A. The New York Giants (1961, 1962) and the Dallas Cowboys (1966, 1967).

Q. Which other team did the '60s Packers defeat for the NFL Championship?

A. The Cleveland Browns (1965).

Q. Which member of the Packers played the most games for the team?

A. Bart Starr (QB, 1956–71) played in 198 games during 16 seasons with the Green and Gold.

Q. What color were the Packers' jerseys in Super Bowl II?

A. White.

Q. Who holds the Packers' record for making the most fair catches in his career?

A. Willie Wood (S, 1960–71), who made 102 fair catches during his years with the team.

Q. Who holds the Packers' record for scoring the most points in a single season?

A. Paul Hornung (RB, 1957–62, 64–66) scored 176 points in 1960.

Q. The 1962 Packers won two games by a margin of 49–0. Which teams did they humiliate by that score?

A. The Chicago Bears and the Philadelphia Eagles.

Q. Who is the only Packers' player to come from Philander Smith College?

A. Elijah Pitts (HB, 1961–69, 71). Pitts was a 13th-round draft choice in 1961.

Q. Which Packers' player scored the most points in a single game?

A. Paul Hornung scored 33 points against the Baltimore Colts on October 8, 1961.

Q. Who holds the Packers' record for scoring the most touchdowns in a single season?

A. Jim Taylor (FB, 1958-66) scored 19 touchdowns in 1962.

Q. Who holds the Packers' single season rushing record?

A. Ahman Green rushed for 1,883 yards in 2003, breaking a record set by Jim Taylor in 1962.

Q. Which Packers' player holds the team record for most career punt returns?

A. Willie Wood (S, 1960–71) returned 187 punts for 1,391 yards during his career with the Packers. He returned two punts for touchdowns, both in 1961.

Q. Which Packers' player holds the record for scoring 100 or more points in a single season?

A. Paul Hornung scored more than 100 points in three seasons: 1960 (176 points), 1961 (146 points), and 1964 (107 points).

Q. Who is the Packers' all-time leading passer?

A. At the end of the 2003 season, QB Brett Favre had completed 3,960 passes in 6,459 attempts for a total of 45,646 yards, 346 touchdowns, and 207 interceptions (1992-2003).

Q. Who is the Packers' all-time leading rusher?

A. Jim Taylor rushed for a career total of 8,207 yards in 1,811 attempts for an average of 4.53 yards per carry.

Q. Which Packers' player had the worst rushing record?

A. Don Horn (QB, 1967–70). In 12 rushing attempts, Horn lost 16 yards, gained 4 yards, and scored one touchdown for a minus 1.00 rushing average.

Q. Which Packers' player holds the record for scoring the most touchdowns in a single game?

A. Paul Hornung scored five touchdowns on December 12, 1965.

Q. Against which team did Hornung score those touchdowns?

A. The Baltimore Colts. Green Bay won, 42–27.

Q. Which Packers' quarterback was sacked the most times in a single game?

A. Bart Starr. The Detroit Lions sacked him 11 times on November 7, 1965.

Q. Which Packers' player returned the most kickoffs for touchdowns during his career?

A. Travis Williams (RB, 1967–70) returned five kickoffs for touchdowns, four of them in his rookie season.

Q. When did the Packers play their first overtime game and who was the opponent?

A. December 26, 1965. The Baltimore Colts.

Q. Which team won that game?

A. Green Bay won that Western Conference Playoff Game 13–10 on a 25-yard Don Chandler (K, 1965–67) field goal.

Q. Which Packers' quarterback has had the fewest passes intercepted in a single season?

A. Bart Starr, who in 1966 had only three interceptions in 251 pass attempts.

Q. Which Packers' player rushed for over 1,000 yards in 5 consecutive seasons?

A. Jim Taylor. Taylor rushed for 1,101 yards in 1960; 1,307 yards in 1961; 1,474 yards in 1962; 1,018 yards in 1963; and 1,169 yards in 1964.

Q. Which Packers' player holds the durability record for playing in the most consecutive games for the team?

A. Quarterback Brett Favre has played in 191 consecutive games (1992-2003), breaking Forest Gregg's record of 187 consecutive games.

Q. Which was Gregg's last NFL team as a player?

A. The Dallas Cowboys.

Q. Who holds the Packers' career record for the most games with 100 yards or more rushing?

A. Jim Taylor, who rushed for 100 yards or more in 26 games.

Q. Who holds the Packers' record of rushing for a touchdown in the most consecutive games?

A. Paul Hornung rushed for TDs in seven consecutive games in 1960.

Q. Who scored the first touchdown in Super Bowl history?

A. Max McGee (WR 1954, 57–67), on a 37 yard pass from Bart Starr.

Q. Who was the oldest man ever to play in a regular season game for the Packers?

A. Ben Agajanian (K, 1961) was 42 when he was acquired to replace regular kicker Paul Hornung (drafted into the military) and backup kicker Jerry Kramer (injured) in 1961.

Q. How many points did Agajanian score as a Packer?

A. Eleven. In three games, Agajanian kicked eight extra points and one field goal.

Q. What is the largest margin of victory in Packers' history?

A. Fifty-three points.

Q. Which team did the Packers score those 53 points against?

A. The Atlanta Falcons. The Packers crushed them 56–3 at Milwaukee, on October 23, 1966.

Q. Who holds the Packers' record for career rushing touch-downs?

A. Jim Taylor, who scored 81 TDs for the Packers.

Q. What color jerseys did the Packers wear in Super Bowl I?

A. Green. The Packers were designated the home team for the first Super Bowl.

Q. What Packers' player of the '60s became famous when he quipped of Coach Vince Lombardi, "He treats us all the same—like dogs."?

A. Henry Jordan (DT, 1959–69), who played nine seasons under Lombardi. Known for his sense of humor, Jordan was inducted into the Green Bay Packer Hall of Fame in 1975 and into the Pro Football Hall of Fame in 1995.

Q. How many members of the Packers' Super Bowl I team have been inducted into the Pro Football Hall of Fame?

A. Nine: Forrest Gregg (RT); Bart Starr (QB); Jim Taylor (RB); Willie Davis (LE); Henry Jordan (RT); Ray Nitschke (MLB); Herb Adderley (LCB); Willie Wood (FS); Coach Vince Lombardi.

Q. Who was named the Most Valuable Player in Super Bowl I and II?

A. Packers' QB Bart Starr.

Q. Nearly everyone knows the Packers won Super Bowls I and II. Where were the games played?

A. Super Bowl I, Memorial Coliseum, Los Angeles; Super Bowl II, the Orange Bowl, Miami.

Q. The Packers played the Oakland Raiders and Kansas City Chiefs in the first two Super Bowls. Which team did they play in which game?

A. Kansas City in Super Bowl I, Oakland in Super Bowl II.

Q. What was the Packers' won-lost record in 1959, the first year that Vince Lombardi was head coach?

A. Lombardi took the team to a 7–5 season, the Pack's first winning season since 1947.

Q. Who was the first defensive player to score in Super Bowl history?

A. Herb Adderley (CB, 1961-1969). In Super Bowl II, Adderley intercepted a pass thrown by Oakland Raiders QB Daryle Lamonica and returned it 60 yards for a touchdown.

Q. Who holds the record for most field goals kicked in one Super Bowl?

A. Packers' kicker Don Chandler kicked four field goals against the Oakland Raiders in Super Bowl II. San Francisco's Ray Wersching tied Chandler's record in Super Bowl XVI (1982), kicking four field goals against the Cincinnati Bengals.

Q. Two members of the Packers' Super Bowl I and II teams played on other winning Super Bowl teams. Who were they?

A. Herb Adderley and Marv Fleming (TE, 1963–69).

Q. On which other Super Bowl teams did Herb Adderley play?

A. The Dallas Cowboys, in Super Bowl VI.

Q. On which other Super Bowl teams did Fleming play?

A. The Miami Dolphins, in Super Bowl VI, VII, and VII.

Q. What were the ticket prices for Super Bowl I?

A. Tickets sold for $6, $10 and $12; still there were 30,000 empty seats in huge Los Angeles Memorial Coliseum.

Q. A one-time only media occurrence took place in Super Bowl I. What was it?

A. The game was televised by two networks—CBS and NBC.

Q. Everyone knows that Bart Starr scored a last second TD to win the 1967 NFL Championship Game against Dallas—forever after known as the "Ice Bowl." Which blockers did he follow into the end zone?

A. Ken Bowman (C, 1964–73) and Jerry Kramer (RG, 1958–68).

Q. Starr's touchdown was one of three the Packers scored in the "Ice Bowl" game. Who scored the others?

A. Boyd Dowler (WR, 1959–69), who caught touchdown passes of eight and 43 yards from Starr.

Q. In 1963, Packers' QB Bart Starr missed four games because of a hairline fracture in his throwing hand. Who was his replacement?

A. QB John Roach (1961–63) filled in for the ailing Starr. Under Roach's leadership, the Packers won three straight games, defeating Baltimore, Pittsburgh, and Minnesota before losing to Chicago.

Q. A pair of Packers who played in the '60s were nicknamed "The Gold Dust Twins." Who were they and why did they acquire the monicker?

A. Donny Anderson (RB, 1966–71) and Jim Grabowski (RB, 1966- 70). The highly touted All-America running backs were paid approximately $1,000,000 (combined) in signing bonuses.

Q. Which Packer player made the most field goals in a single playoff game?

A. Don Chandler kicked four field goals against the Oakland Raiders in Super Bowl II.

Q. How many TD passes did Bart Starr throw in 1959, Vince Lombardi's first year as the Packers' head coach?

A. Six. He was second to QB Lamar McHan (1959–60) who threw eight TDs.

Q. Which team did the Packers defeat in Lombardi's first victory as head coach and what was the score?

A. Green Bay downed the Chicago Bears 9–6 on September 27, 1959.

Q. Who was named Packers' head coach when Vince Lombardi resigned in 1968?

A. Phil Bengtson, who had coached the Packers' defense under Lombardi.

Q. What was the Packers' record in Bengtson's first year as head coach?

A. The team went 6–7–1, suffering their first losing season since 1958, the year before Lombardi arrived on the scene.

Q. Which Packers' kicker holds the team record for the longest punt in a game?

A. Don Chandler, who kicked a 90-yard punt against the San Francisco 49ers on October 10, 1965.

Q. When was the Packers' first ever game with the Dallas Cowboys?

A. November 13, 1960, at Green Bay. The Packers won, 41–7.

Q. Which Green Bay Packer played in the most post-season games?

A. QB Brett Favre has played in 19 post season games.

Q. Which Green Bay player holds the record for most career punts in postseason play?

A. Donny Anderson, who punted 20 times in four post-season games.

Q. Who scored Green Bay's first TD in the Packers' first play-off game against the Dallas Cowboys?

A. Elijah Pitts scored the first TD in the 1966 NFL Championship Game against the Cowboys on a 17-yard pass from Bart Starr.

Q. Which veteran of five Packer championship teams and two Super Bowls did not play football until his junior year in college?

A. Fred "Fuzzy" Thurston (G, 1959–67). A native of Altoona, Wisconsin, Thurston first played football at Valparaiso University.

Q. Who was the Packers' backup quarterback during the glory years of the Vince Lombardi era?

A. Edmund (Zeke) Bratkowski (QB, 1963–68, 71). In regular season play, Bratkowski completed 220 of 416 pass attempts for 3,147 yards and 21 touchdowns.

Q. What is Bart Starr's full name?

A. Bryan Bartlett Starr.

Q. Which Packer player did Vince Lombardi trade on the spot when he showed up for contract negotiations with an agent?

A. Jim Ringo (C, 1953–63). When Ringo arrived in Lombardi's office with an agent, Lombardi excused himself. Returning shortly, he told Ringo that he'd been traded to the Philadelphia Eagles. Ringo is a member of both the Green Bay Packer Hall of Fame and the Pro Football Hall of Fame.

Lynn Dickey—great passer, little protection. Vernon J. Biever photo.

CHAPTER SIX

Hard Times at Lambeau Field
The 1970s and '80s

The winning legacy left by Vince Lombardi withered in the 1970s and '80s as a succession of coaches (four), quarterbacks (many) and non-winning seasons (17 of 20) gave the Packer faithful precious little to cheer about.

The Packers became the NFL's whipping boys, and Green Bay came to be regarded as a frozen hell-hole where NFL coaches threatened to send players who didn't perform.

There were occasional bright spots. The Packers made the playoffs in 1972 and '82. Quarterback Lynn Dickey passed for 4,458 yards in an 8–8 season (1983), and led the Pack in a wild and wooly shoot-out that is still the highest scoring game ever played on Monday Night Football.

But for every highlight there were a dozen low points and the Packers of the '70s and '80s labored mostly in obscurity. As the 1980s faded into history, the ghost of Vince Lombardi hung over Lambeau Field like a curse.

Q. Which player scored the most points in his rookie season with the Packers?

A. Chester Marcol (K, 1972–80) scored an NFL-leading 128 points in 1972.

Q. Which Packer player gained the most yards in his rookie season?

A. John Brockington (RB, 1971–77) ran for 1,105 yards in 216 attempts in 1971 and scored four rushing touchdowns.

Q. Which Packer holds the team record for career kickoff returns?

A. Steve Odom (WR, 1974–79), who returned 179 kickoffs for 4,124 yards and two touchdowns during his six-year career.

Q. What was Odom's longest return?

A. Ninety-five yards.

Q. What is the Packers' record for most fumbles in a single season?

A. The Pack fumbled 44 times in 1988.

Q. Which Packer quarterback was sacked the most times during his career?

A. In 12 seasons with the Packers, Brett Favre has been sacked 366 times, breaking QB Lynn Dickey's record of 268 sacks.

Q. Who was the Packers' first Monday Night Football opponent?

A. The San Diego Chargers, at San Diego, on October 12, 1970.

Q. Who won the game?

A. Green Bay won, 22–20.

Q. Who led the Packers in both rushing and receiving in the 4–10–0 season of 1977?

A. Barty Smith (FB, 1974–80) gained 554 yards and scored two TDs in 166 rushing attempts, and caught 37 passes for 340 yards and one TD.

Q. Which Packers' quarterback was sacked the most times in a single season?

A. Don Majkowski (QB, 1987–91) was sacked 47 times in 1989.

Q. Which member of the Green Bay Packers' Hall of Fame and the Pro Football Hall of Fame spent most of his playing years with Kansas City?

A. Jan Stenerud (K, 1980–83) spent 13 years with the Kansas City Chiefs. In four years with the Packers, Stenerud scored 292 points (115 extra points, 59 field goals).

Q. Against which team did the Packers play their longest ever game (including overtime)?

A. The Detroit Lions, on October, 11, 1987. The Packers lost the four-hour, nine-minute game at Green Bay in overtime, 19–16.

Q. Against which team did the Packers play their longest non-overtime game?

A. The Detroit Lions, on November, 27, 1986. The Packers won the three-hour, 43-minute marathon at Detroit by a score of 44 to 40. The Packers also played a three-hour, 41-minute game against the Lions at Detroit on November 12, 1989, which the Lions won 31–22.

Q. Green Bay holds the NFL record for the most overtime games played in a single season. How many games was that?

A. Five.

Q. What was the year and who were the Packers's overtime opponents?

A. The year was 1983. The Packers defeated Houston 41–38 and Tampa Bay 12–9. They lost to Minnesota 20–17, Detroit 23-20, and Atlanta 47–41.

Q. In 1983, the Packers played the game with the highest combined score in franchise history. What team did they play and what was the score?

A. The Packers downed the Washington Redskins in a 48–47 Monday night shootout at Lambeau Field October 17, 1983. The game featured 11 touchdowns, 11 extra points, and six field goals, and was also the highest scoring game ever played on Monday Night Football.

Q. Who scored the winning points in that game?

A. Jan Stenerud kicked the winning field goal.

Q. Which Packers' quarterback has had the most passes intercepted in a single season?

A. Lynn Dickey had 29 of 484 attempts intercepted in 1983.

Q. Which player holds the Packers' record for the most rushing attempts in a single game?

A. Terdell Middleton (RB, 1977–81) rushed 39 times for 110 yards in a game against the Minnesota Vikings on November 26, 1978.

Q. Which Packers' quarterback holds the career team record for the most 300-yards-or-more passing games?

A. Until Brett Favre surpassed his mark in 1997, Lynn Dickey held the record of passing for 300 or more yards in 15 games.

Q. Until Brett Favre upped the ante to seven, in 1995, which Packer quarterback held the single-season record for most games passing for 300 or more yards?

A. Don Majkowski threw for 300 yards or more in six games in 1989.

Q. Which Packers player turned a blocked kick into a sudden-death victory for the Packers?

A. Chester Marcol. On September 7, 1980, Marcol's field goal attempt against the Chicago Bears was blocked, but the ball bounded back into his arms. Marcol scampered 25 yards for a TD, giving the Packers a 12–6 overtime victory.

Q. In the 10–6 season of 1989, the Packers set an NFL record for one-point victories. How many games did they win by that margin?

A. Four.

Q. Who were the teams Green Bay defeated by a single point?

A. New Orleans 35–34, Chicago 14–13, Minnesota 20–19, and Tampa Bay 17–16.

Q. Curly Lambeau had the longest tenure as player / coach with the Packers. Who had the next longest?

A. Dave Hanner, who was with the Packer organization for 28 years.

Q. What position did Hanner play with the Packers?

A. Defensive tackle. He played in 160 games (1952–64).

Q. In what capacity did Hanner serve the Packers when his playing days ended?

A. Defensive line coach (1965–71) and defensive coordinator (1972–79).

Q. Which Packers' player was nicknamed the "Polish Prince"?

A. Placekicker Chester Marcol.

Q. What is the largest point deficit the Packers have overcome to win a game?

A. Twenty-three points. The Pack was down 23–0 and won 35–23.

Q. Against which team did they accomplish this?

A. The Los Angeles Rams, in a game played at Milwaukee on September 12, 1982.

Q. In the decade of the '70s, Packers' players rushed for 1,000 yards or more in four seasons. Who were they?

A. John Brockington rushed for 1,105 yards (216 attempts) in 1971; 1,027 yards (274 attempts) in 1972; and 1,144 yards (265 attempts) in 1973. Terdell Middleton rushed for 1,116 yards (284 attempts) in 1978.

Q. Two players with the same name played for the Packers at the same time in 1976. Who were they?

A. Mike McCoy. Mike P. McCoy, defensive tackle from Notre Dame, played in 96 games for the Packers from 1970–76. Mike C. McCoy, corner back from Colorado, played in 110 games from 1976–83.

Q. Who is the Packers' all-time QB sack leader?

A. Tim Harris (LB, 1986–90) had a total of 55.0 sacks and led the team in sacks in each of his five seasons with the Packers.

Q. The Packers gave up a two-game total of 60 points against the same team in 1970 and failed to score in either game. Who was that team?

A. Detroit. The Lions trounced the Packers 40–0 in the season opener at Green Bay and pounded the Packers 20–0 in the season finale at Detroit.

Q. Packers' head coach Phil Bengtson resigned two days after the 1970 season ended. Who was hired to replace him?

A. Dan Devine (1971–73).

Q. An unusual thing happened to Devine in his very first game as the Packers' head coach. What was it?

A. Devine was run over by a group of players in the season opener and suffered a broken leg.

Q. Green Bay scored 40 points in the 1971 season opener and still lost the game. Who did they play and what was the final score?

A. The New York Giants, who won 42–40.

Q. Packers' QB Bart Starr retired in July, 1972. Who replaced him as Green Bay's starting quarterback?

A. Scott Hunter (1971–73), the Packers' sixth-round draft choice in 1971.

Q. Coach Devine started three different quarterbacks in the 1973 season. Who were they?

A. Scott Hunter, Jim Del Gaizo (1973), and Jerry Tagge (1972-74).

Q. Which of the these three threw the most touchdown passes?

A. The '73 QB race was a study in mediocrity. Hunter, Del Gaizo, and Tagge each threw just two TD passes.

Q. In 1974, Dan Devine gave up two first-round draft picks, two seconds, and a third-round draft pick to obtain what he hoped would be a winning QB. Who was that player?

A. Thirty-four year-old Los Angeles Rams QB John Hadl (1974-75). In seven games that year, Hadl threw three of the Packers' five TD passes.

Q. Former Packers' superstar QB Bart Starr was hired to replace Dan Devine at the end of the 1974 season. In nine years as the Packers' head coach, how many non-losing seasons did Starr produce?

A. Three. Under Starr's guidance the Packers were 8–7–1 in 1978, 8–8 in 1981 and 5–3–1 in 1982.

Q. Because of a players' strike during the 1982 season, seven of the Packers' regular season games were canceled and one was moved to January, 1983. Which game was moved?

A. The Packers-Lions game, originally scheduled for November 14, was moved to January 2. Detroit won, 27–24.

The Packers sneaked into the playoffs in 1982 for the first time in a decade and were 1–1 in postseason play. Who were their opponents?

A. The St. Louis Cardinals, whom the Packers trounced 41–16, and the Dallas Cowboys, who defeated Green Bay 37–26.

Q. Which was the worst defensive year in Packers' history?

A. The 1983 Packers' defense gave up 6,403 yards and 439 points, both team records.

Q. What was the injury that ended QB Lynn Dickey's playing career?

A. He injured his neck while working out on a nautilus machine with three games left in the 1985 season, and never played again.

Q. What is the team record for most fumbles in a single game?

A. The Pack fumbled eight times in two games; against Philadelphia on December 1, 1974, and against Tampa Bay on December 7, 1988.

Q. What is the greatest number of penalties the Packers have incurred in a single season?

A. The Green and Gold drew 135 penalties in 1987.

Q. Who holds the Packers' record for most kickoff returns in a single season?

A. In 1998, Roell Preston returned 57 kickoffs for 1,497 yards and two touchdowns.

Q. What was the worst season start in Green Bay history?

A. Under head coach Forrest Gregg (1984–87), the Packers lost their first six games in 1986.

Q. What did Packer players Dale Dawson, Dean Dorsey, and Curtis Burrow have in common?

A. All were Packers' placekickers during the 1988 season. Together they accounted for four of nine field goals and six of 10 extra points.

Q. Forrest Gregg left the Packers at the end of the 1987 season. Who replaced him as head coach?

A. Lindy Infante.

Q. In how many seasons of his illustrious career with the Packers did QB Bart Starr fail to complete a touchdown pass?

A. Only one, 1971. Hampered by injuries, Starr started only three games in 1971. He completed 24 of 45 pass attempts for 286 yards and three interceptions.

Q. The Packers were 10–4 in 1972 and made it to the playoffs for the first time since Super Bowl II, then lost the NFC Conference Playoff Game to the Washington Redskins. Who scored Green Bay's only points in that game?

A. Chester Marcol kicked a 17-yard field goal. Washington won 16–3.

Q. In two games in 1980 the Packers gave up 112 points while scoring only 28. Who were their opponents in those games?

A. The Los Angeles Rams, who whipped the Packers 51–21 on September 21, and the Chicago Bears, who humiliated Green Bay 61–7 on December 12.

Q. One of the bright spots for the Packers in the '70s and '80s was James Lofton (WR, 1978–86). In how many seasons did Lofton have more than 1,000 yards receiving?

A. Five: 1980 (1,226 yards, four TDs); 1981 (1,294 yards, eight TDs); 1983 (1,300 yards, eight TDs); 1984 (1,361 yards, seven TDs); and 1985 (1,153 yards, four TDs).

Q. Which Packer was nicknamed the "Majik Man?"

A. QB Don Majkowski, who thrilled fans with his wild scrambles, "Hail Mary" passes, and come-from-behind victories during the Packers' 10–6 season in 1989. He was the first Packers' QB named to the Pro Bowl since Bart Starr in 1966.

Q. What is the record number of safeties scored against the Packers in a single game?

A. Two. Los Angeles Rams' defensive end Fred Dryer sacked Packers' quarterbacks Scott Hunter and Jim Del Gaizo in the end zone in the Rams' 24–7 victory over the Packers on October 21, 1973.

Q. Which Packers' QB holds the record for most consecutive passes completed in a single game?

A. The record is 18, shared by Lynn Dickey (against the Houston Oilers on September 4, 1983) and Don Majkowski (against the New Orleans Saints on September 17, 1989). The Packers won both games.

Q. Which Packer player holds the team record for the longest touchdown made from a fumble recovery?

A. Scott Stephen (LB, 1987–91), who returned a fumble 76 yards for a touchdown against the Chicago Bears on December 17, 1989.

Q. What is the Packers' record for most consecutive games lost at Green Bay (since 1933)?

A. Eight, 1985–87.

Q. Which Green Bay player holds the record for the most punts in his career?

A. David Beverly (P, 1975–80), who punted 495 times in six seasons with the Packers.

Q. What's the largest number of points the Packers have scored in a postseason game?

A. The Packers downed the St. Louis Cardinals 41–16 in the 1982 NFC First-Round Playoff Game.

Super offense. Super season. Super Bowl. Vernon J. Biever photo.

CHAPTER SEVEN

Return to Glory
The 1990s

Although the decade of the '90s got off to a rocky start (the Packers were 6–10 in 1990 and 4–12 in 1991), the skies above Lambeau Field began to brighten when Ron Wolf was hired as Green Bay's general manager, on November 27, 1991. Lindy Infante was fired as Packers' head coach in late December, and the New Year was barely under way when San Francisco 49ers offensive coordinator Mike Holmgren was hired as the Green Bay Packers' eleventh head coach.

In February, 1992, the Packers sent a first-round draft pick to the Atlanta Falcons for a quarterback named Brett Favre, then picked receiver Robert Brooks, running back Edgar Bennett, and tight end Mark Chmura in the 1992 draft. By the start of the season, nearly half of the Packers' 1991 roster had been replaced.

Despite a few glitches—the Packers won only three of their first nine games—Wolf and Holmgren produced a winning team in 1992. And the best was yet to come.

Q. In 1995, a Packer player rushed for more than 1,000 yards for the first time in 17 years. Who was that player and for how many yards did he rush?

A. Edgar Bennett (RB, 1992–96) rushed for 1,067 yards.

Q. Who is the Packers' all-time leading receiver?

A. Sterling Sharpe (WR, 1988–94) caught 595 passes for 8,134 yards and 65 touchdowns.

Q. Who holds the Packers' record for the longest field goal?

A. Chris Jacke kicked a 54-yard field goal against the Detroit Lions on January 2, 1994. Ryan Longwell tied Jacke's record with a 54-yarder against Tennessee on December 16, 2001.

Q. In 1992, the Packers put together a six-game winning streak. How long had it been since the team had won six games in a row?

A. Twenty-seven years. The 1965 Packers won the first six games of the regular season.

Q. More than any other Packers' head coach, Mike Holmgren has been compared to the legendary Vince Lombardi. In the first 34 games of their careers at Green Bay, which coach had the better record at Lambeau Field?

A. Holmgren's record was 30–4; Lombardi's 28–6.

Q. Who holds the Packers' record for most passes completed in a single game?

A. Brett Favre completed 36 passes in a game on December 5, 1993.

Q. Who was the Packers' opponent in that game?

A. The Chicago Bears.

Q. Who won that game?

A. The Bears won, 30–17.

Q. Which Green Bay player holds the team record for most pass receptions in a single postseason game?

A. Edgar Bennett had nine receptions in the 1993 Divisional Playoff Game against the Dallas Cowboys.

Q. Green Bay holds the NFL record for number of consecutive post season games won at home, which is?

A. Ten.

Q. Which team did the Packers defeat to give Mike Holmgren his first victory as Green Bay's head coach?

A. The Cincinnati Bengals, in Game 3 of the '92 season.

Q. Who caught Brett Favre's TD pass to give Green Bay the 24-23 victory?

A. Kittrick Taylor (WR, 1992).

Q. Who holds the single game record for most passing yards at Lambeau Field?

A. Joe Montana. On November 4, 1990, the then San Francisco quarterback threw for 411 yards. The 49ers downed Green Bay, 24–20.

Q. Who did the Packers defeat for their first playoff victory under Coach Mike Holmgren?

A. The Detroit Lions. The Packers defeated the Lions 28–24 at Detroit, one week after losing the regular season finale at Detroit.

Q. How many quarterback sacks did Reggie White (DE, 1993–96) have in his first season with the Packers?

A. White had 13 QB sacks in 1993.

Q. The 1993 Packers sacked opposing quarterbacks 46 times and gave up 30 QB sacks to their opponents. Before then, when was the last time Green Bay had more QB sacks than their opponents?

A. In 1984, when the Packers had 44 QB sacks and gave up 42.

Q. Which team traded Brett Favre to Green Bay?

A. The Atlanta Falcons. The trade came on February 10, 1992.

Q. When was the first Green Bay-Atlanta game after the Packers acquired Favre and who won?

A. October 4, 1992, at Atlanta. The Falcons won, 24–10.

Q. Which '90s Packer player once "mooned" a TV news helicopter?

A. Jim McMahon (QB, 1995–96). The incident occurred in 1986 when McMahon was the Bears' QB.

Q. In four seasons as Green Bay's back-up quarterback behind Brett Favre, how many game situation passing attempts did Ty Detmer have?

A. Twenty-one. Detmer signed with the Philadelphia Eagles as an unrestricted free agent in 1996.

Q. Defensive end Reggie White led the Packers with 13 sacks in 1993. Who was the Pack's sack leader in 1994?

A. Sean Jones (DE, 1994–96) led the 1994 Packers with 10.5 sacks.

Q. Who was the Packer punter in 1996?

A. Craig Hentrich (P, 1994-96).

Q. Who provides the cheerleaders for the Packers' home games?

A. Since the early '90s, cheerleaders from the University of Wisconsin-Green Bay have led the cheers at Packers' home games. They are introduced at Lambeau Field as the UW- Green Bay cheerleaders and are not listed in the game program.

Q. In 1992, wide receiver Sterling Sharpe set an NFL record for pass receptions. How many passes did he catch?

A. Sharpe's 108 receptions was an NFL record. His 1,461 yards and 13 touchdowns were also league records.

Q. Who holds the Packers' record for most field goals kicked in a single game?

A. Placekicker Chris Jacke kicked five field goals in two games—against the Los Angeles Raiders (1990) and the 49ers (1996). Ryan Longwell kicked 5 field goals against Arizona on September 24, 2000.

Q. Who holds the Packers' record for most kickoff returns in his rookie season?

A. Charles Wilson (WR, 1990–91) returned 35 kickoffs for 798 yards in 1990.

Q. The Packers gave up a record number of sacks in 1990. How many were there?

A. Sixty-two.

Q. The Packers' 1990 rushing leader was Michael Haddix (RB, 1989–90), who gained how many yards?

A. Haddix gained 311 yards rushing, the lowest for a team leader since 1958.

Q. Who was the Packers' rushing leader in 1958?

A. Paul Hornung led the '58 Packers' rushing attack with 310 yards.

Q. Lindy Infante, the Packers' head coach for four seasons (1988–91) had a record of 24–41, for a winning percentage of .375. Who was the last Packers' head coach to have a winning percentage that low or lower?

A. Ray (Scooter) McClean (1958), whose 1–10–1 record was .125 percent.

Q. Despite his bleak overall record, Infante led the Packers to a 10–6 season in 1989. When was the last time before then that the team had a winning season?

A. 1978. Green Bay was 8–7–1.

Q. Despite going 4–12 in 1991, the Packer defense allowed opponents an average of only 96.6 yards rushing per game. When was the last time the Packers held opposing teams to so few rushing yards?

A. The 1940 Packers allowed only 94.5 rushing yards per game.

Q. In 1990, Packer QB Don Majkowski was injured in Game 10 against the Phoenix Cardinals. Who was his replacement?

A. Anthony Dilweg (QB, 1989–90).

Q. Dilweg was 1–2 before he was injured in the Philadelphia game. Who replaced him?

A. Blair Kiel (QB, 1990–91), who went 0–3 for the season.

Q. Wide receiver Sterling Sharpe caught 67 passes for 1,105 yards and six TDs in 1990. In terms of pass receiving yards, who was the Packers' number two receiver that year?

A. Perry Kemp (WR, 1988–91), who caught 44 passes for 527 yards and two touchdowns.

Q. Who was the Packers' leading QB in 1991?

A. Mike Tomczak (QB, 1991), who completed 128 of 238 pass attempts for 1,490 yards and 11 touchdowns.

Q. In his brief stint with Green Bay, Tomczak led the Packers' quarterback corps in all categories but one, which was?

A. Sacks. In 1991, Don Majkowski was sacked 30 times for 152 yards, Tomczak 13 times for 152 yards, Blair Kiel twice for 13 yards.

Q. Who led the team in QB sacks during Holmgren's first year as head coach?

A. Tony Bennett (LB, 1990–93), who had 13.5 sacks in 1992.

Q. The Packers had 46 QB sacks in 1993. When was the last year they sacked opposing quarterbacks that many times?

A. In 1965 Green Bay sacked opposing QBs 48 times.

Q. In 1995 Brett Favre became the third Packers quarterback in franchise history to complete 1,000 or more passes. Who were the others?

A. Bart Starr (1,808) and Lynn Dickey (1,592).

Q. Who was the Packers leading punt returner in 1991?

A. Val Sikahema (RB, 1991), who returned 26 punts for a total of 239 yards.

Q. Who holds the Packers' record for scoring the most consecutive points after touchdown?

A. Kicker Chris Jacke kicked 134 consecutive PATs 1990–94.

Q. Which NFL team was Ron Wolf working for when he was hired as the Packers's general manager?

A. Wolf was director of player personnel for the New York Jets.

Q. Which other coach was in the running when Mike Holmgren was hired as the Packers' head coach?

A. Bill Purcells, who at the time decided not to return to coaching.

Q. What is Packer's QB Brett Favre's middle name?

A. Lorenzo.

Q. When did the Packers play their last game in Milwaukee?

A. December 18, 1994.

Q. Who was their opponent and who won the game?

A. The Atlanta Falcons. Green Bay won 21–17 on a last second rushing TD by QB Brett Favre.

Q. Which Packer players of the '90s attended the following small colleges in Illinois: a) Western Illinois; b) Eastern Illinois; c) Illinois State; d) Millikin?

A. a) Frank Winters (OL, 1992–96), b) John Jurkovic (NT, 1991–94); c) Mike Prior (S, 1993–96); d) Jeff Query (WR, 1989–91).

Q. Which Green Bay player of the late '90s was nicknamed "The Minister of Defense?"

A. Defensive end Reggie White.

Q. Quarterback Brett Favre's 77 TD passes in the 1995 and '96 seasons rank second to which other NFL QB in a two-year span?

A. Miami's Dan Marino, who threw 78 touchdown passes in 1984 and '85.

Q. Who scored Green Bay's only touchdown in the 1994 Divisional Playoff Game against Dallas?

A. Edgar Bennett, on a one-yard run.

Q. Who holds the Packers' record for the longest pass interception returned for a TD in postseason play?

A. George Teague (S, 1993–96) returned a pass interception for an NFL-postseason record 101 yards and a TD in the 1993 NFC Wild Card Game on January 8, 1994.

Q. Who was the Packers' opponent and who won the game?.

A. The Detroit Lions. Green Bay won, 28–24, for its first playoff win in 11 years.

Q. Who holds the Packers' record for most receiving touchdowns scored in a single season?

A. Sterling Sharpe caught 18 touchdown passes in 1994.

Ray Nitschke, all-time Packer great, spanned the years 1958–1972.
Vernon J. Biever photo.

CHAPTER EIGHT

Spanning the Years

This is a time traveller chapter, where most questions bridge more than one or two decades of Packer history. Others are here just for the fun of it.

Q. Including postseason play, how many Packers' coaches have had winning records?

A. Only three: Curly Lambeau, 1921–49 (212–106–21); Vince Lombardi, 1959–67 (89–30–4), and Mike Holmgren, 1992–96 (57–32–0).

Q. What do Packers Ron Widby (P, 1972–73), John Losch (HB, 1956), Fred Provo (B, 1948), Dennis Claridge (QB, 1965), Bob Nussbaumer (B, 1946, '51), and Sterling Sharpe (WR, 1988–94) have in common?

A. Each completed 100 percent of their career pass attempts. Widby (2 attempts), Losch (1 attempt) and Provo (1 attempt) each threw for a touchdown.

Q. Which Green Bay Packer attended medical school part-time during his playing days and became a doctor when his football career ended?

A. Malcolm Snider (G, 1972–74). Snider attended medical school at the University of Wisconsin-Madison on off days during the playing season and full time during the off season. Today he is an orthopedic surgeon.

Q. How many Packers have returned kickoffs for more than 100 yards?

A. Five: Al Charmichael (HB, 1953–58), 106 yards; Herb Adderly (CB, 1961–69), 103 yards; Travis Williams (RB, 1967–70), 104 yards; Dave Hampton (RB, 1969–71), 101 yards; Roell Preston (WR/KR, 1998), 101 yards.

Q. How many men whose last names began with the letter "Q" have played for the Green Bay Packers?

A. Three: Jess Quatse (T, 1933), Jeff Query (WR, 1989–91), and Bill Quinlan (DE, 1959–62).

Q. The Packers have retired four numbers in franchise history—No. 3, 14, 15, and 66. Which players wore those numbers?

A. Tony Canadeo (3); Don Hutson (14); Bart Starr (15); and Ray Nitschke (66).

Q. Who were the first Packer players inducted into the Pro Football Hall of Fame in Canton, Ohio?

A. Earl (Curly) Lambeau (founder, player, coach, 1919-1949), Robert (Cal) Hubbard (T, 1929–35), Don Hutson (E, 1935–45), and Johnny (Blood) McNally (HB, 1928–36) were inducted into the Pro Football Hall of Fame in 1963.

Q. Who was the tallest head coach in Packer history?

A. Mike Holmgren tops the lineup at 6-feet, 5-inches.

Q. While coaching high school football in California, Packer coach Mike Holmgren also taught what subject?

A. History.

Q. Which Packer players also became head coaches for the Green and Gold?

A. Curly Lambeau (1919–49), Bart Starr (1975–83), and Forrest Gregg (1984–87).

Q. Which Packer player scored the most rushing touch-downs in his rookie season?

A. Three players share the record of five touchdowns: Charles (Buckets) Goldenberg (B / E, 1933–45), 1933; Gerry Ellis (FB, 1980–86), 1980; Brent Fullwood (FB, 1987–90), 1987.

Q. The Packers are the only publicly-owned team in the NFL. How many shareholders are there?

A. A non-profit corporation, the Packers are owned by 111,507 stockholders who own 4,748,910 shares of stock. Just try to move that team from Green Bay!

Q. How many Packers' first-round draft picks have come from the University of Wisconsin?

A. Three: Ed Jankowski (B), 1937; George Paskvan (B), 1941; Earl (Jug) Girard (QB), 1948.

Q. Four of the six longest punts in Packers' history were kicked by two players. Who were they?

A. Jack Jacobs (QB, 1947–49), 78 yards against the Chicago Cardinals in 1948 and 74 yards against the Rams in 1947; Boyd Dowler (WR, 1959–69), 75 yards against the Vikings in 1961 and 75 yards against the 49ers in 1962.

Q. Over the years, the longest punts in Packer history were all kicked in the same month. Which month was it?

A. October. Don Chandler, 90 yards, October 10, 1965; Jack Jacobs, 78 yards, October 10, 1948; Boyd Dowler, 75 yards, October 22, 1961 and October 21, 1962; Arnie Herber, 74 yards, October 22, 1939; and Jack Jacobs, 74 yards, October 5, 1947.

Q. What is placekicker Chester Marcol's real first name?

A. Czeslaw.

Q. Over the years, how many men named Smith have played for the Green Bay Packers?

A. Twenty-two: Barry (WR, 1973-75); Barty (RB, 1974-80); Ben (E, 1933); Blane (G, 1977); Bruce (LB, 1945-48); Donnell (DE, 1971); Earl (E, 1922); Ed (HB, 1948-49); Ed (B, 1937); Ernie (T, 1935-37, 39); Jermaine (DT, 1997, 99); Jerry (G, 1956); Kevin (FB, 1996); Larry (DT/DE, 2003); Moe (RB, 2002); Ollie (WR, 1976-77); Perry (DB, 1973-76); Red (G, 1927, 29); Rex (E, 1922); Rod (CB, 1998); Warren (G, 1921); Wes (WR, 1987).

Q. What is the fewest number of first downs the Packers have conceded to an opponent in a single game?

A. Although held without a first down, the New York Giants defeated the Packers 10–7 on October 1, 1933.

Q. The 1996 Packers scored 56 touchdowns in regular season play. What was the record for regular season TDs before then?

A. The 1962 Packers scored 53 regular season touchdowns.

Q. Who was the last Packers' player with no college affiliation?

A. Lineman Greg Jensen, who played one game on the Packers' "replacement team" in the strike-shortened season of 1987. The last regular season player with no college affiliation was running back Charlie Leigh, who played 12 games for the Packers in 1974.

Q. Which Packer player was nicknamed the "Gray Ghost of Gonzaga?"

A. The famed Tony Canadeo, who was prematurely gray in his 20s. The name was a combination of his hair color and his alma mater, Gonzaga University.

Q. Who was the first Heisman Trophy winner drafted by the Packers?

A. Paul Hornung, who won the award during his senior year at Notre Dame.

Q. There is a unique distinction to Hornung's Heisman Trophy award. What is it?

A. Hornung is the only Heisman Trophy winner to have played for a losing team the year he won the award.

Q. What did Packers' quarterback Irv Comp and defensive back Bobby Dillon have in common?

A. Comp (1943–49) and Dillon (1952–59) each had sight in only one eye.

Q. Despite their vision limitations, both players set team records. What were they?

A. Irv Comp had ten interceptions in six games in 1943 and holds the team record for interceptions in his rookie year. Dillon holds the Packers' record for career interceptions with 52.

Q. Vince Lombardi resigned as Packers' head coach at the end of the 1967 season. How many winning seasons did the team have over the next quarter-century?

A. Six: In 1969, 1972, 1978, 1982, 1989, and 1992.

Q. What was the Packers' best record during that time period?

A. The team was 10–6–0, in 1989.

Q. What was the Packers' worst record during that time period?

A. A dismal 4–12–0, in 1988.

Q. Who were the father and son who played for the Packers 17 years apart?

A. Elijah Pitts (HB, 1961–69, 71) and Ron Pitts (DB, 1988–90). Elijah played 126 games for the Packers, while Ron played 44, making four interceptions.

Q. Which Green Bay player took up acting after his football career ended and has been featured in top TV and film roles?

A. Carlos Brown (QB, 1975–76). Under the stage name Carlos Autry, he has been featured in the TV series "Grace Under Fire" and "In the Heat of the Night," and in such films as "Amazing Grace and Chuck," "Southern Comfort," "North Dallas Forty," and "Popeye."

Mike Sherman takes the reins.
Vernon J. Biever photo.

CHAPTER NINE

Changing the Guard
Entering the 21st Century

The Packers lost a heartbreaker in the NFC Wild Card playoff game at San Francisco on January 3, 1999; five days later Head Coach Mike Holmgren resigned to become head coach and general manager of the Seattle Seahawks.

Ray Rhodes, former Eagles head coach and ex-Packer defensive coordinator was then named Packers head coach. But after a lackluster 8-8 season that saw the Pack miss the playoffs for the first time in six years, Rhodes was dismissed.

Mike Sherman, Seattle's offensive coordinator and a 21-year coaching veteran, became the Packers' thirteenth head coach in January 2000. Ron Wolf retired as Packers executive vice president and general manager in February of 2001, and Sherman was named to succeed Wolf as general manager in addition to his coaching duties.

Brett Favre signed a "lifetime" contract with the Packers in February 2001, assuring that he will finish his playing career with Green Bay. And on May 19, 2001, a ceremonial ground breaking marked the beginning of a major Lambeau Field renovation.

Q. Who holds the team record for most opponent's fumbles recovered for a touchdown?

A. Keith McKenzie (DE, 1996–99) recovered three fumbles for Packer TDs.

Q. What was McKenzie's longest recovered fumble return?

A. McKenzie returned a fumble for 88 yards and a TD against the Pittsburgh Steelers on November 9, 1998.

Q. A low point in the 1999 season was the game at Tampa Bay, when the Packers produced the fewest rushing yards in a game, which was?

A. Twelve yards in 12 carries.

Q. Who were the Packers' rushing leaders in the game?

A. Dorsey Levens (RB, 1994–2001), 10 yards in 4 carries, and Brett Favre, 2 yards in 8 carries.

Q. The 1999 season also produced a 1,000-yard rusher. Who was he?

A. Dorsey Levens, who rushed for 1,034 yards in 279 carries.

Q. How many 300-yard passing games did Brett Favre have in 1999?

A. Six.

Q. What was Favre's highest passing yardage game in 1999, and his lowest?

A. Favre passed for 390 yards and 2 TDs against Tampa Bay at Green Bay, and 120 yards and no TDs at Denver.

Q. The final game of the 1999 season was held on January 2, 2000. Who did the Packers play?

A. Arizona at Green Bay.

Q. Mike Sherman led the Packers to a 9–7 season during his first year as head coach. Who were the Packs' first victims?

A. The Packers downed the Philadelphia Eagles at Green Bay on September 17 by a score of 6–3 on the strength of two Ryan Longwell (K, 1997–) field goals.

Q. How many games did the Packers win on the road?

A. Three. They defeated the Arizona Cardinals 29–3, the Chicago Bears 28–6, and the Minnesota Vikings, 33–28.

Q. Which Packer holds the record of most games rushing 100 yards or more in a single season?

A. Ahman Green (RB, 2000-) rushed for 100 or more yards in 10 games in 2003.

Q. Who holds the record for scoring the most TDs in a single game?

A. Paul Hornung (B, 1957-62, 64-66) scored five touchdowns at Baltimore on December 12, 1965).

Q. Which Packer holds the record for most combined net yards gained in a single season?

A. Ahman Green gained 1,981 combined yards (1,387 rushing, 594 receiving) in 2001.

Q. Which Packers receiver caught touchdowns in the most consecutive games in the 2001 season?

A. Receiver Bill Schroeder (WR, 1994, 97–01) caught TDs in four consecutive games.

Q. Who was the Packers' sack leader for the 2001 season?

A. Kabeer Gbaja-Biamila (DE, 2000–) had 13.5 sacks.

Q. Can you name the Packers player who has caught the most playoff games passes in his career?

A. Antonio Freeman (WR, 1995–2001) caught 47 passes in 12 playoff games.

Q. Which Packers receiver holds the team record for one or more receptions in consecutive playoff games?

A. Dorsey Levens has snared at least one pass in 12 consecutive playoff games.

Q. Who holds the Packers' record for the most fair catches in a single season?

A. Allen Rossum (CB/KR, 2000–2001) made 21 fair catches in the 2000 season.

Q. Only three players in Packers history have rushed for 1,000 yards in two or more consecutive seasons. Who were they?

A. Jim Taylor (1961–64), John Brockington (1971–73) and Ahman Green, who rushed for 1,175 yards in 2000, and 1,387 yards in 2001.

Q. What is the record for total yardage in kickoff returns for the Packers?

A. The Pack returned 64 kickoffs for a record 1,570 yards in the 2000 season, an average of 24.5 yards per return.

Q. How many times have the Packers faced the San Francisco 49ers in playoff competition?

A. Five: in 1996, 1997, 1998, 1999, and 2002.

Q. How did the Packers fare?

A. Green Bay won the NFC Divisional Playoff on Jan.6, 1996, by a 27–17 score; the NFC Divisional Playoff on January 4, 1997 by 35–14; the NFC Championship on January 11, 1998 by 23–10; and the NFC Wildcard playoff on January 13, 2002 by 25–15. Green Bay lost the NFC Wildcard playoff on January 3, 1999 by 30–27.

Q. Who was named the Packers' most valuable player for the 2001 season?

A. Ahman Green who, in his third season with the Packers, racked up 1,981 total yards from scrimmage and caught 62 passes.

Q. How many touchdowns did Green make in 2001?

A. Eleven: 9 rushing and 2 receiving.

Q. Green Bay's 2001 season came to a bitter end when they lost the NFC Divisional Playoff game to St. Louis 45–17. The game set a Packers record, which was?

A. It was the worst playoff loss in team history.

Q. Brett Favre also set a record in that game, which was?

A. Favre threw six interceptions (3 for TDs) which set a team record for most interceptions in a playoff game.

Q. How many times did the Packers punt in the two 2002 playoff games?

A. Six, 3 against San Francisco on January 13, and 3 against St. Louis on January 20.

Q. Who holds the record for the most yards gained on kickoff returns in playoff games?

A. Antonio Freeman, who returned kickoffs for 413 yards in 10 playoff games.

Q. The Packers 35-20 loss to New Orleans on September 15, 2002 produced a statistical rarity. What was it?

A. Both teams had 357 net yards of offense.

Q. In that same game, one of Brett Favre's most celebrated streaks came to an end. What was it?

A. New Orleans' Darrin Smith intercepted Favre's fifth pass of the day, ending his string of consecutive passes without an interception at 158.

Q. The Packers and Bears have played 164 regular season games in their long rivalry. How long have they been playing and who leads the series?

A. At the end of 2002, 81 years. The Bears led the series 83 to 75; there have been 6 ties.

Q. In the Packers 28-10 defeat of New England in week six of the season, Ahman Green set a team record. What was it?

A. Green surpassed 3,000 rushing yards in his Packers career. Reaching the goal in 37 games, he became the fastest in the team history to reach the 3,000 yard mark.

Q. Who held the record before Green?

A. John Brockington (RB 1971-77) held the previous "fastest" honor, reaching the 3,000 yard mark in 40 games.

Q. Brett Favre added another laurel to his illustrious career in the New England game. What was it?

A. With three touchdown passes, Favre's total reached 301, surpassing John Elway's 300, and elevating him to third in scoring passes in pro football history.

Q. As the Packers defeated Buffalo 10-0 in week 16 of the season, Vonnie Holiday (DE 1998-2002) set a team record by sacking Bills' quarterback Drew Bledsoe five times. Who was the previous record holder?

A. Linebacker Bryce Paup (1990-94) had four sacks against Tampa Bay in 1991. The Packers' Ezra Johnson had five sacks against Detroit on Sept. 3, 1978, but the league didn't begin officially counting sacks until four years later.

Q. The Packers split with the Vikings in 2002, losing 31 to 21 at Minnesota and winning 26 to 22 at Green Bay. After 83 games, how did the rivalry stand?

A. The series was dead even. Each team had won 41 games and there was a 10-10 tie in 1978.

Q. In the Packers' victory over New England on October 13, 2002, Brett Favre passed for 147 yards and moved into seventh place in all-time career passing yardage with 40,244 yards. What legendary quarterback did he surpass?

A. The late Johnny Unitas, who ended his NFL career with 40,239 passing yards.

Q. Until the Packers' 27-7 loss to Atlanta at Lambeau Field on January 4, 2003, the Pack had never lost a home playoff game since the NFL instituted post season in 1933. How long was their winning streak?

A. The Packers were 13-0 at home, with 11 victories at Lambeau and two in Milwaukee.

Ahman Green slices through the Viking defense on his way to a record-setting season.
Vernon J. Biever photo.

CHAPTER TEN

A Game Of Heart

The 2003 season began with a 9-0 loss to Kansas City in a lightning-shortened Pro Football Hall of Fame game at Canton, Ohio, and ended with an overtime playoff loss to the Eagles that squashed the Packers' Super Bowl hopes.
In between, the Pack went 10-6, won the NFC North Championship, beat the Bears twice, lost the home opener (which rededicated the magnificently renovated Lambeau Field) to the Vikings and sneaked into the playoffs thanks to a last-second Arizona Cardinals' TD that gave Green Bay the division championship.

Brett Favre's father passed away on December 21. At Oakland the next evening, before a national TV audience, Farve led the Packers to a 41-7 rout of the Raiders, passing for 399 yards and four TDs.

When it was over, Farve and his wife, Deanna, walked off the field arm in arm, headed for Mississippi.

Yes, it is a game of heart.

Q. The renovated Lambeau Field now has 72,515 seats. How many did the stadium seat when it opened in 1957?

A. 32,150.

Q. How long is the Kentucky bluegrass at Lambeau Field?

A. One and one-eighth inches. The field is mowed every other day.

Q. Which is the most popular sandwich at Packer home games, brats or hot dogs?

A. Hot dogs. An average of 10,650 is served at each game, while the average number of brats is 7,900.

Q. Lambeau Field was called new City Stadium when it opened in 1957. When was it given its present name?

A. It was renamed Lambeau field on Sept. 11, 1965, following the death of Curly Lambeau.

Q. Counting all games the Pack has played since the team was founded in 1919, what is the team's winning percentage?

A. .576. The Packers have won 832 games, lost 608 and played to 48 ties.

Q. The Packers-Titans preseason game at Lambeau began on August 28, 2003 and ended the next day. Why?

A. The Thursday night game was suspended in the second quarter for two hours and 33 minutes due to torrential rains and lightning. It ended at 12:47 A.M. Friday.

Q. Who won the game?

A. The Titans won 23-7.

Q. How many other games at Lambeau Field have been suspended?

A. It's believed to be the first game suspended since Lambeau Field opened in 1957.

Q. Name the Packer player who holds the team record for most consecutive punts with none blocked.

A. Josh Bidwell (P, 2000-2003) has punted 308 consecutive times with none blocked.

Q. Which Packer player holds the record for most punts in a single game?

A. Two players share the record of 11 punts in a single game: Clarke Hinkle (FB, 1932-41) against Chicago on December 10, 1933, and Jug Girard (B, 1948-51) against the Bears on October 15, 1950, and against Los Angeles on December 3, 1950.

Q. It is common Packer trivia knowledge that Don Chandler kicked the longest punt in team history— 90 yards against San Francisco in 1965. Who kicked the second longest punt in Packer history?

A. Jack Jacobs (B, 1947-49) kicked a 78-yarder against the Chicago Cardinals in 1948.

Q. Both players made those kicks on the same date, although 17 years apart. What was it?

A. October 10.

Q. The Packers beat the Bears twice in 2003. What is Brett Farve's record against the Bears?

A. 20-4.

Q. The Packer victory against Tampa Bay on November 16, 2003 was Brett Farve's 120th as a starter, moving him into fourth place on the NFL career wins list. What player did he move above?

A. The revered Hall of Famer, Johnny Unitas.

Q. What players does Farve trail on the career victory list?

A. John Elway (148), Dan Marino (147), and Fran Tarkenton (125).

Q. Three Packer players share the record for most rushing TD's in a single game. Who are they?

A. Jim Taylor (FB, 1958-66) at Cleveland, 1961; at Chicago, 1962; at Philadelphia, 1962. Terdell Middleton (RB, 1977-81) against Seattle, 1978, and Dorsey Levens (RB, 1994-2001), against Arizona, 2000.

Q. And the record number of TD's is?

A. Four.

Q. The kickoff temperature for the Arizona game on September 21, 2003 equaled the hottest game ever for the Packers. How hot was it?

A. 102 degrees at kickoff.

Q. In the Packers-Seahawks game at Green Bay on October 5, 2003, Seattle kicker Josh Brown kicked the longest field goal ever scored against the Packers. How long was it?

A. 58 yards.

Q. What is Brett Farve's record in domed stadiums?

A. Following the Lions game at Detroit on November 22, 2003, Farve's domed stadium record stood at 13-22.

Q. The Pack ran the ball 48 times in the November 23, 2003 victory over the 49ers, the most in more than 20 years. When was the last time the team ran that many times?

A. The Packers ran the ball 49 times against the New York Giants on October 4, 1981.

Q. Brett Farve's four touchdowns against the Oakland Raiders on December 22, 2003, gave him 345 TD's and second place on the NFL's career touchdown list. Who did he pass and who does he trail?

A. Favre passed Frank Tarkenton and trails only Dan Marino (420).

Q. Who holds the team record for most rushing TD's in a season?

A. Ahman Green, who scored two TD's against Denver on December 28, 2003, giving him 20 for the season and breaking Jim Taylor's record of 19 set in 1962.

Q. When Al Harris (CB, 2003) intercepted Seahawks' QB Matt Hasselbeck's pass in the Packer's-Seahawks overtime playoff game on January 1, 2004 and ran for a TD, he set an NFL record. What was it?

A. It was the first defensive TD to win an overtime playoff game in NFL history.

Q. Who holds the Packers' record for most rushing attempts in a single season?

A. Ahman Green rushed 355 times in 2003 (16 games), breaking Dorsey Levens' record set in 1997.

Q. Name the Packer player who holds the record for most seasons leading the league in pass interceptions.

A. Three Packers led the league in pass interceptions for one year: Don Hutson (1940, 10 games), Willie Wood (1962, 14 games), and Darren Sharper (2000, 16 games).

Q. Which Packer scored the most TD's on pass interceptions in his rookie year?

A. Darren Sharper (CB/S, 1997-2003) two TD's in 1997, and Marques Anderson (S, 2002-03) two TD's in 2002.

Q. How many Packer players have been inducted into the Pro Football Hall of Fame?

A. As of the end of the 2003 season, 20 Packers are members of the Hall of Fame.